Published By
MEREDITH MUSIC PUBLICATIONS
a division of G.W. Music, Inc.

MEREDITH MUSIC PUBLICATIONS and its stylized double M logo are trademarks of
Meredith Music Publications, a division of G.W. Music, Inc.

Cover design by John Heinly

ISBN: 1-57463-005-9

November 1981
First Edition

FOREWORD

The purpose of this text is to provide a comprehensive course of study for the beginning timpanist. This volume contains all of the fundamental elements of timpani playing. Included are technical studies that deal with single strokes, the roll, muffling, staccato, cross sticking, and tuning. The musical studies beginning on page 34, are based on a variety of materials that include simple to intricate rhythmic combinations; a varied use of time signatures, tempi, marks of expression and tuning; and musical styles ranging from early classical to syncopated swing. Tuning studies provide a unique introduction to this important aspect of timpani playing. Diagrams are used throughout to help the student clearly understand each fundamental technique.

It is my sincere hope that Primary Handbook for Timpani will provide an enjoyable and educationally rewarding approach to timpani playing.

G.W.

to my family—
ADELE, MEREDITH, and GAR,
with love

INTRODUCTION

CONTENTS

This text is designed to provide the beginning timpani student with a complete course of study utilizing all of the fundamental techniques for timpani. The text is divided into two parts. The first part deals specifically with technique and tuning. The second part is comprised of thirteen musical studies complete with performance suggestions. These studies enable the student to apply in a musical context, the techniques from part one. The thirteen musical studies are also suitable for recital or conest. Included in this volume are:

SINGLE STROKE STUDIES—These studies will enable the student to develop a strong fundamental technique and a good, musical sound. They also provide adequate time for correct muscle development before greater technical demands confront the student. Sticking indications are provided to establish correct playing procedures.

ROLL STUDIES—The roll studies progress in difficulty beginning on drums tuned to pitches requiring only slow and relaxed rolls. The graduation of studies allows adequate time for necessary muscle development before fast or short rolls appear.

MUFFLING STUDIES—This unique technical requirement of timpani playing is approached using very simple exercises that allow the student to concentrate on muffling. The studies cover all aspects of muffling two drums.

STACCATO STUDIES—These studies are designed to develop both loud and soft staccato strokes. All fundamental facets of staccato playing are covered.

CROSS STICKING STUDIES—The purpose of these studies is to develop complete control of cross sticking. Both right over left and left over right sticking is developed.

TUNING STUDIES—A short tuning study is included on each page of part I. Each study requires the student to tune the timpani, play several measures, retune, and complete the exercise on the retuned drums. The studies begin very simply using a fermata to provide unlimited time to tune one drum. They then progress in difficulty and finally require the retuning of both drums within a prescribed period of time. These studies are extremely important and can provide a solid foundation in tuning.

PRACTICE CHART—To reinforce the need for consistent study a practice chart is provided at the bottom of each page. Students should be encouraged to record their practice time daily. Requesting parents to sign the practice chart will provide additional reinforcement.

PERFORMANCE FUNDAMENTALS

CLEF—Music for timpani is written in the bass or F clef. Memorize the following clef and all the notes including those above and below the staff.

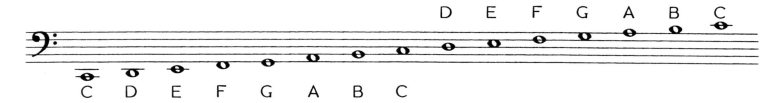

RANGE—A basic set of timpani consists of two drums that measure 28 and 25 inches in diameter. Advanced literature often requires the use of three or four drums. The additional drums are usually 23 and 30 inches. The normal playing range of a set of four timpani is diagramed below.

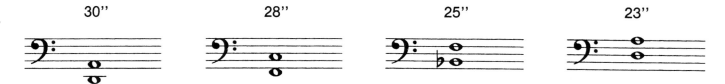

TUNING—The ability to accurately tune the timpani is an essential performance technique. To begin, the student must develop the ability to identify and sing all intervals that occur within an octave both ascending and descending. This is best accomplished by (1) learning to sing each interval using the keyboard to check for accuracy and, (2) using a sight-singing method to further develop the ability to sing intervals in context. Many teachers approach intervals by associating the interval with the first two notes of a familiar tune. Tunes often used in this method include the following:

Interval: Major second
Tune: "Alouette"

Interval: Major third
Tune: "Marine's Hymn"

Interval: Perfect fourth
Tune: "Here Comes The Bride"

Interval: Perfect fifth
Tune: "Twinkle, Twinkle Little Star"

Interval: Major sixth
Tune: "My Bonnie Lies Over The Ocean"

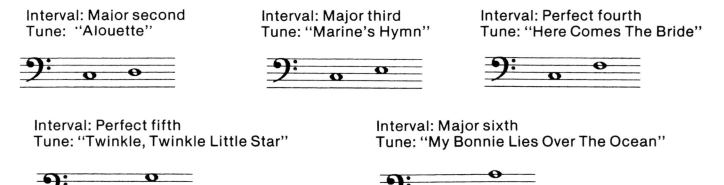

Once the ability to identify and sing intervals has been mastered the student should be capable of tuning the timpani using the following system:

(1)   Release the head tension on all drums to be tuned.
(2)   Sing the lowest pitch to be tuned.
(3)   Gently strike the drum.
(4)   Slowly increase the tension on the head by pushing down on the pedal until the desired pitch is reached.
(5)   Using this note as the root, sing the interval to the next drum and repeat the procedure in #3 and #4.

At first a pitch pipe should be used to ascertain the initial pitch. As the student progresses the pitch pipe should be replaced with an A-440 tuning fork. The student should be encouraged to memorize this pitch by listening to the tuning fork and singing the A-440.

It is often necessary to change the pitch of one or more drums during a period of rest. This change is accomplished by singing the interval between the existing pitch and the pitch to be tuned and following the previously outlined procedure for tuning. It is often necessary to count rests while changing pitch. This process is developed in Part I of the text.

STICKS—Most professional timpanists use at least six different pairs of sticks. A variety of sticks is necessary to produce the many nuances of sound required by today's repertoire. It is not uncommon in fact, for a timpanist to have several sets of sticks from which to choose. In this case the final selection of sticks is often based on the acoustical characteristics of the performance hall. The student timpanist should have at least three pairs of sticks to adequately perform the basic band or orchestral literature. These sticks should consist of:

(1)   Small, hard felt headed sticks for precise rhythms and staccato effects.
(2)   Medium size, felt headed sticks for general purpose playing.
(3)   Large size, soft felt or cartwheel sticks for full tone and legato playing.

GRACE NOTES—When written for timpani grace notes are executed using single, alternating strokes. Grace notes are played "open" so as not to choke the drum head. The following illustrates the correct method of performing the three most common grace note figures written for timpani:

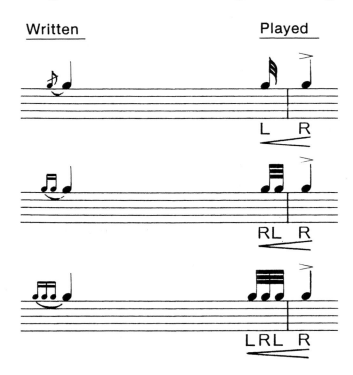

GLISSANDO—A characteristic idiom for timpani is the glissando (gliss). This special effect is produced by striking the drum and pedaling up or down to the indicated pitch. The following are common methods of notating the glissando:

Ascending

Descending

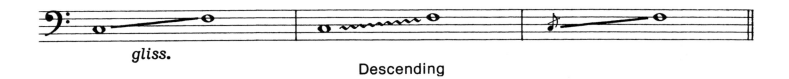

SINGLE STROKE STUDIES

HAND POSITION—The timpani stick is held between the first joint of the index finger and the pad (fleshy part) of the thumb. This point of contact is approximately four inches from the end of the stick. The third finger should make contact with the stick as it is used to guide and generate the stick's motion. The fourth and fifth fingers normally do not touch the stick. The grip of both hands is the same.

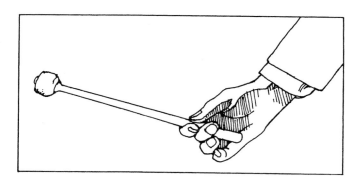

PLAYING POSITION—Many timpanists stand while playing. It is not incorrect however, to sit on a high stool especially when playing pieces that require rapid tuning changes. The choice of whether to stand or sit is a personal one. Regardless, the performer must be in a position close enough to the drums to easily strike the beating spot without extending the arms. The sticks are held several inches above and parallel to the head. By holding the elbows out slightly, away from the sides of the body, the heads of both sticks will angle in directly over the beating spot.

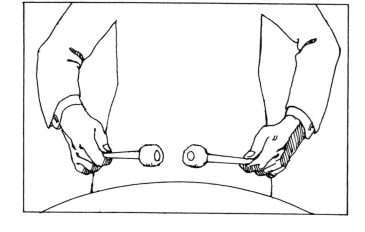

THE STROKE—The normal, often called, legato stroke is a relaxed motion with a complete follow-through. This stroke begins with the stick parallel to the drum head. Using the wrist, raise the head of the stick approximately twelve inches from the drum head. With a slight downward motion, allow the stick to drop to the drum head and bounce back to its position approximately twelve inches above the drum. The entire stroke should consist of one smooth and continuous motion. The legato stroke is used to "pull" as much tone from the drum as possible. Note: the height or size of the stroke is determined by the dynamic level of the music. The louder the dynamic level, the larger the stroke. The full twelve inch stroke will enable the student to develop the legato stroke with complete freedom of motion.

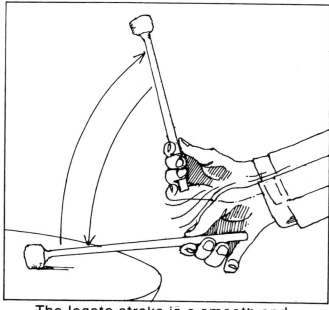

The legato stroke is a smooth and continuous motion.

PLAYING AREA—The playing area or beating spot is between three and four inches from the rim. Always strike the same area to produce a consistent sound.

STICKING—Generally, all strokes on timpani are alternated (i.e., LRLR or RLRL). Doubling and cross sticking should be avoided whenever possible (see Cross Sticking Studies, page 30). As a general rule try to keep the left and right hands on their respective low and high drums. In order to establish correct sticking technique, the following studies include all sticking indications.

Tuning Study

Technical Studies

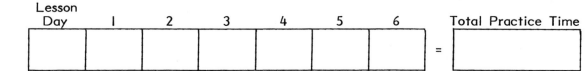

Record your practice time for each day of the week.

Lesson Day	1	2	3	4	5	6	Total Practice Time
							=

Tuning Study

Technical Studies

	Lesson Day	1	2	3	4	5	6		Total Practice Time
Record your practice time for each day of the week.								=	

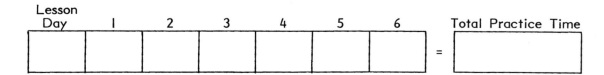

Tuning Study

Technical Studies

	Lesson Day	1	2	3	4	5	6		Total Practice Time
Record your practice time for each day of the week.								=	

Tuning Study

Technical Studies

	Lesson Day	1	2	3	4	5	6		Total Practice Time
Record your practice time for each day of the week.								=	

Tuning Study

Technical Studies

	Lesson Day	1	2	3	4	5	6		Total Practice Time
Record your practice time for each day of the week.								=	

Tuning Study

G-C

G to F

Technical Studies

G-C

RLR LRL   LRL RL   RL   RLRLRL   RLR LRL   RLRLRL

RLRLRL   LRLRLR   RLR   RLR   RLR   RLR RLR   RL   RL

RL   LR   LR   LR   RLRLRL   RLRLRL   RLR LRL RL   RL

R L R L RLRL R   LR   RL   RLRL R   R L R L

LRLR L   RLR   RLR   RLRL R   R RL   R RL LR   LR   R RL

R RL LRLR   R   L R   L R   LRLR L   LRL   RLR   LRLR   R

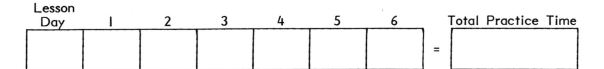

	Lesson Day	1	2	3	4	5	6		Total Practice Time
Record your practice time for each day of the week.								=	

Tuning Study

Technical Studies

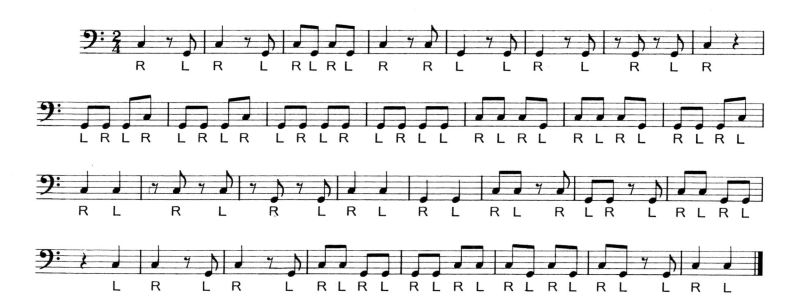

Lesson Day	1	2	3	4	5	6		Total Practice Time

Record your practice time for each day of the week.

ROLL STUDIES

The purpose of the roll is to evenly sustain a sound. The roll is produced by alternating single strokes, the speed of which is determined by the amount of tension on the head. The tighter the head (higher the pitch), the faster the speed of the roll must be. To produce a smooth roll, relaxed legato strokes are used; no articulation should be heard. Hard sticks should not be used since they produce an articulated staccato effect. A smooth roll will occur when the head is kept vibrating at an even speed.

The dynamic level of the roll is determined by the size of the stroke, not the speed of the stroke. The louder the roll, the larger the stroke. When making a crescendo or decrescendo roll, only the size (height) of the strokes will be altered.

Size, not speed determines the dynamic level of the roll.

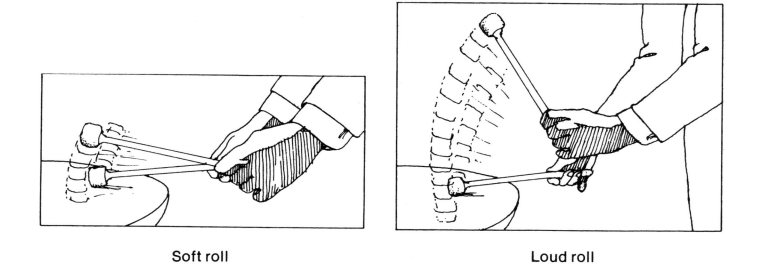

Soft roll   Loud roll

Roll notation varies from one historical period to another and from one composer to another. Rolls are usually notated in one of the following ways:

(1)   Three slashes above or below a note

(2)   A trill indication

(3)   Notes from two drums connected by three slashes indicating a simultaneous roll on both drums (one hand on each drum).

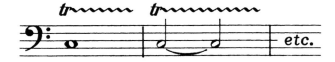

Practice the following exercises using both loud and soft dynamic levels.

Tuning Study

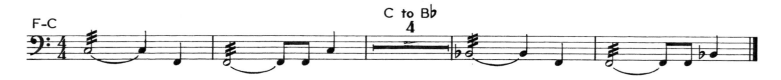

Technical Studies

Record your practice time for each day of the week.	Lesson Day	1	2	3	4	5	6		Total Practice Time
								=	

Tuning Study

G to B♭

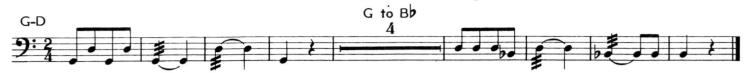

Technical Studies

Record your practice time for each day of the week.	Lesson Day	1	2	3	4	5	6		Total Practice Time
								=	

Tuning Study

Technical Studies

	Lesson Day	1	2	3	4	5	6		Total Practice Time
Record your practice time for each day of the week.								=	

Tuning Study

Technical Studies

Record your practice
time for each day of
the week.

Lesson Day	1	2	3	4	5	6		Total Practice Time
							=	

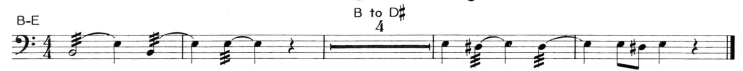

Tuning Study

Technical Studies

19

Record your practice time for each day of the week.	Lesson Day	1	2	3	4	5	6	=	Total Practice Time

Tuning Study

Technical Studies

Lesson Day	1	2	3	4	5	6		Total Practice Time
							=	

Record your practice time for each day of the week.

Tuning Study

Technical Studies

Record your practice time for each day of the week.

Lesson Day	1	2	3	4	5	6		Total Practice Time
							=	

MUFFLING STUDIES

The purpose of muffling the timpani head (i.e., stopping the sound) is to control the duration of sound and/or to stop one sound from interfering with another. To muffle, simply press on the drum head where it was struck using the third, fourth, and fifth fingers. Press hard enough to stop the sound but not hard enough to change the pitch. Do not slap the drum when muffling. There are two ways to muffle, either with the same hand that strikes the drum or with the free hand.

Muffling is usually indicated by a rest. However, since composers are not consistent with this aspect of timpani notation rests do not always indicate muffling. Listening and developing an awareness of musical style is the most intelligent approach to learning when to muffle.

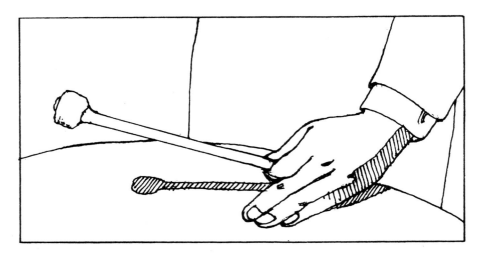

Use the third, fourth, and fifth
fingers to muffle the drum head.

EXAMPLES OF MUFFLING:

Muffling to control the duration of sound.

Muffling to control one sound from interfering with another.

Practice muffling the following using: (1) The same hand that
strikes the drum.
(2) The free hand.

(1) R (R) R (R) R (R) R (R)   L (L) L (L) L (L) L (L)
(2) R (L) R (L) R (L) R (L)   L (R) L (R) L (R) L (R)

Tuning Study

Technical Studies

Record your practice time for each day of the week.

Lesson Day	1	2	3	4	5	6		Total Practice Time
							=	

Tuning Study

Technical Studies

Lesson Day	1	2	3	4	5	6		Total Practice Time
							=	

Record your practice time for each day of the week.

Tuning Study

Technical Studies

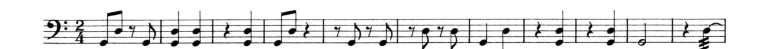

Record your practice time for each day of the week.

Lesson Day	1	2	3	4	5	6		Total Practice Time
							=	

STACCATO STUDIES

The staccato stroke is used to articulate rhythmic figures that, due to low register and/or rhythmic drive, need to be reinforced. This stroke is produced by a quick, snapping wrist motion and by increasing the pressure of the grip between the thumb and index finger. The degree of staccato (i.e., stroke size and pressure of the grip) is determined by the dynamic level. Use the following as a guide:

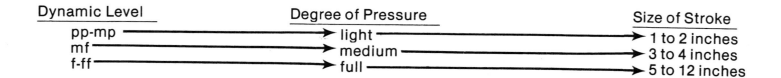

Dynamic Level	Degree of Pressure	Size of Stroke
pp-mp	light	1 to 2 inches
mf	medium	3 to 4 inches
f-ff	full	5 to 12 inches

A staccato effect may also be produced by muffling or by placing a felt muting device on the drum head. The use of small, hard felt headed sticks will also produce a staccato effect. However, it is not always possible to use this type of stick when staccato playing is necessary. The student should develop the staccato stroke so that it may be used whenever required and with any type of stick.

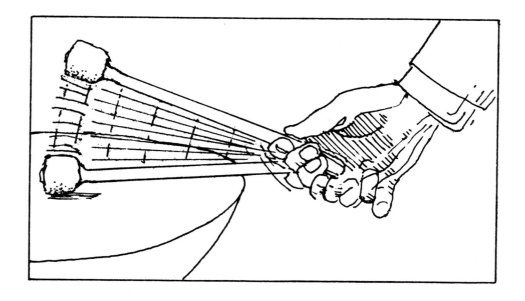

Use a quick, snapping wrist
motion for the staccato stroke.

Play the following exercises using the staccato stroke. Determine the degree of staccato by the dynamic level indicated.

Tuning Study

Technical Studies

	Lesson Day	1	2	3	4	5	6		Total Practice Time
Record your practice time for each day of the week.								=	

Tuning Study

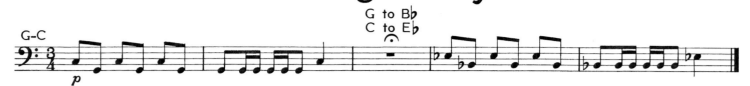

Technical Studies

Record your practice time for each day of the week.	Lesson Day	1	2	3	4	5	6		Total Practice Time
								=	

Tuning Study

Technical Studies

	Lesson Day	1	2	3	4	5	6		Total Practice Time
Record your practice time for each day of the week.								=	

CROSS STICKING STUDIES

The purpose of using cross sticking (one stick crossing over the other) is to enable the performer to play fast, articulate rhythmic figures using single strokes. The use of single strokes produces a clean, even sound that is not normally possible using double sticking. Cross sticking should be used only when there is a musical demand such as the need to move rapidly between two or more drums.

When cross sticking, be sure to keep both hands close together using a conservative motion. Strike the head on the normal beating spot with a straight--not glancing--stroke. The sign ⊗ indicates the point at which the cross sticking occurs.

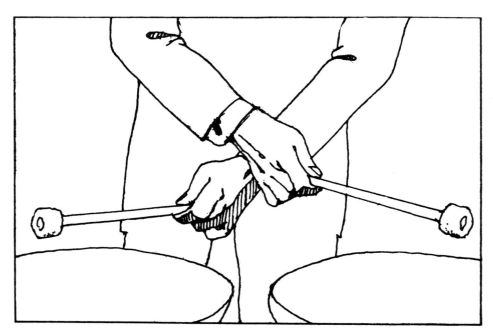

Keep both hands close together
when cross sticking.

Practice and memorize the following cross sticking patterns until they are easily playable at ♩ = 120.

Right hand cross

Left hand cross

Tuning Study

G to B
C to E

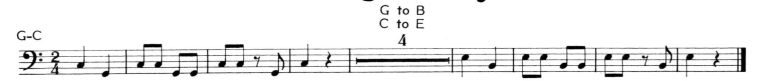

Technical Studies

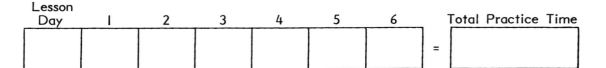

	Lesson Day	1	2	3	4	5	6		Total Practice Time
Record your practice time for each day of the week.								=	

Tuning Study

A to F
D to Bb

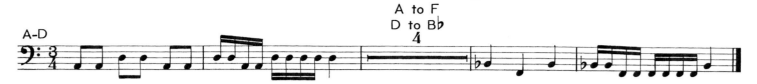

Technical Studies

Record your practice time for each day of the week.	Lesson Day	1	2	3	4	5	6		Total Practice Time
								=	

Tuning Study

Technical Studies

Record your practice time for each day of the week.	Lesson Day	1	2	3	4	5	6	=	Total Practice Time

PART II—MUSICAL STUDIES

The following musical studies are based on technical and tuning skills developed in Part I of this text. The studies are characteristic of band, orchestral, and solo literature for timpani. They include simple to intricate rhythmic combinations; a varied use of time signatures, tempi, marks of expression, and tuning; and musical styles ranging from early classical to syncopated swing. Each solo is a complete musical work.

When learning this material, the student is expected to analyze each piece in order to determine the correct application of technique. Correct sticking, muffling, type of stroke, and dynamic nuance should all be considered. When necessary, the student should write in the selected sticking, rhythmic syllable, and whatever else is needed to insure a successful performance. In addition to study material, these solo studies may be used for student auditions, recitals, or contests.

The following glossary presents terms that are contained in the solo studies.

GLOSSARY

Expression

Pianissimo (pp)—very soft.
Piano (p)—soft.
Mezzo forte (mf)—moderately loud.
Forte (f)—loud.
Forte Piano (fp)—accent strongly, instantly diminish to piano.
Accent (>)—accent or mark the note.
Crescendo ⬤——————◼ —gradually louder.
Decrescendo or Diminuendo ◼————◤ —gradually softer.
Espressivo (esp.)—with expression.
Morendo—dying away.
Sforzando (sfz)—an intense, sudden accent.

Miscellaneous

Al fine—to the end.
Allargando—a broadening of the tempo (growing slower).
Double stop—from violin playing meaning two strings together adapted here to mean both drums together.
Fermata (⌒)—a hold or pause.
Luftpausa (//)—a sudden pause.
Molto—very much.
Ritardando (rit.) — a gradual slowing of the tempo.
Sempre—always.
Sub-divide—to divide the rhythm into smaller divisions for rhythmic accuracy.

This solo contains dynamic indications that must be carefully restated throughout. Use the staccato stroke to articulate all sixteenth note rhythms. Subdivide dotted rhythms. Use general purpose or staccato sticks.

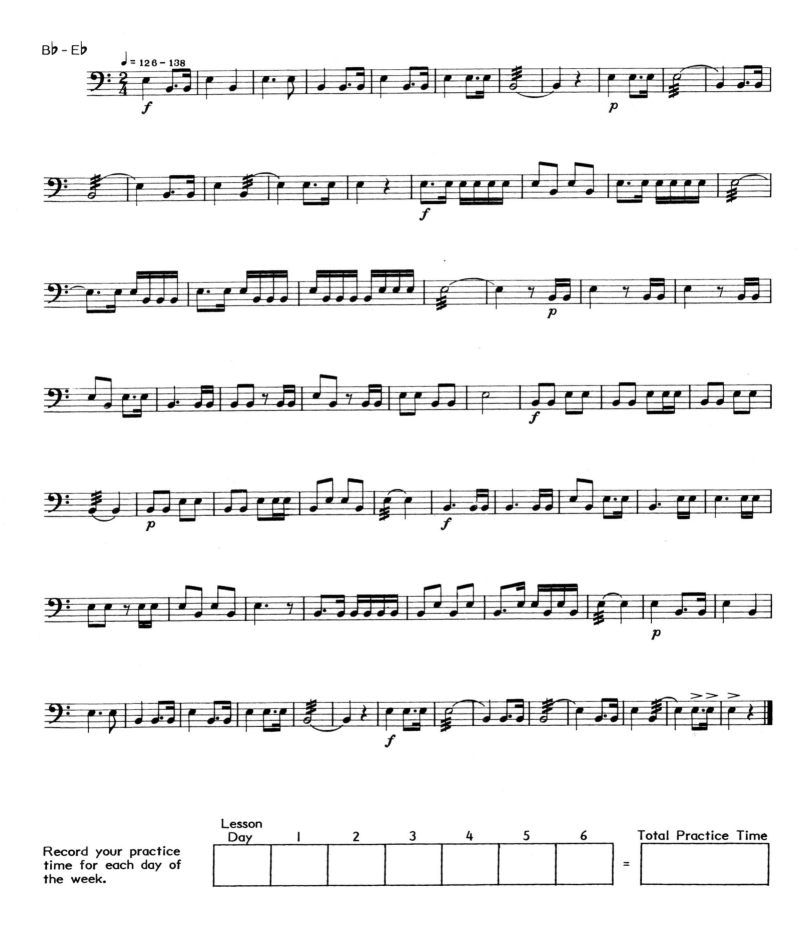

Lesson Day	1	2	3	4	5	6		Total Practice Time
							=	

Record your practice time for each day of the week.

This study requires excellent control in order to maintain a soft dynamic level throughout (*sempre*). The performer must listen carefully to make sure that both drums are dynamically balanced. Use general purpose sticks.

Record your practice time for each day of the week.

Lesson Day	1	2	3	4	5	6		Total Practice Time
							=	

Dynamic balance may be a problem in this study since the high drum often predominates when timpani are tuned in wide intervals. Be aware of this problem and control the volume of the high drum. Play this study using the staccato stroke to insure clean articulation. Use staccato sticks.

F-F

Record your practice time for each day of the week.

Lesson Day	1	2	3	4	5	6	Total Practice Time
							=

38

This rhythmically active study requires staccato strokes and careful selection of sticking. Notate any difficult sticking patterns, especially those requiring cross sticking. Be careful to play the triplets and dotted figures with precise rhythmic accuracy. Use staccato sticks.

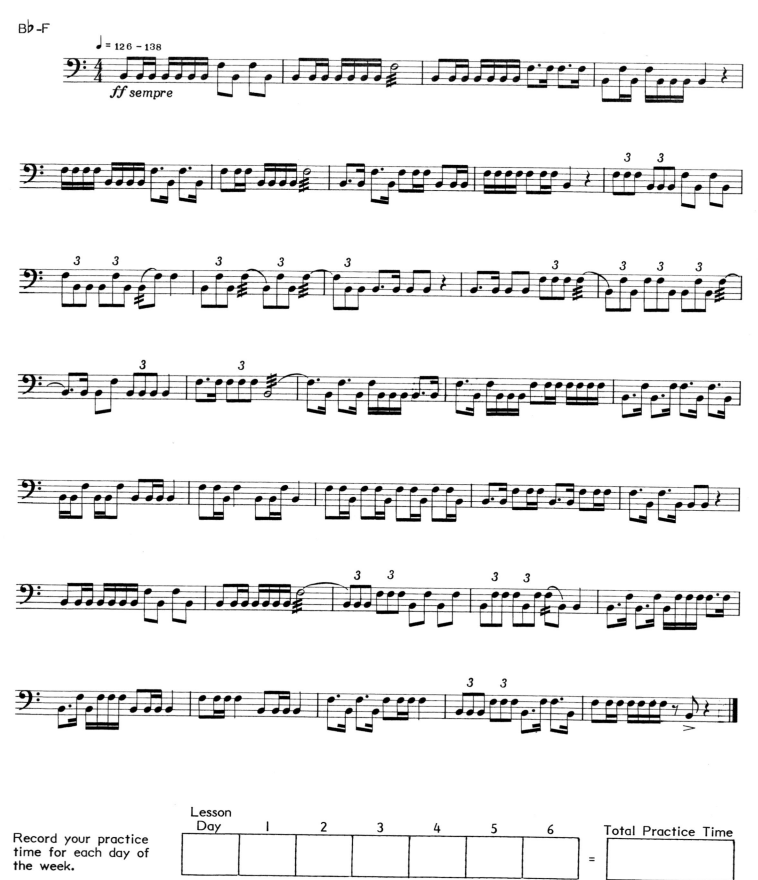

Play this study in an energetic, staccato style. *Sforzando* (*sfz*) is an intense accent played in relation to the dynamic level in which it occurs. The *sforzando* accents should be louder than the accents in measure eight. Use staccato sticks.

When playing this study, emphasize the tonal quality of the timpani by "drawing" the sound from the drums. Make sure that the double stops are played together; they must not sound like grace notes. Be careful to observe the *espressivo* in measure twenty and the *luftpausa* in measure fifty-three. Use general purpose sticks.

C-D

Record your practice time for each day of the week.

Lesson Day	1	2	3	4	5	6		Total Practice Time
							=	

Play this study feeling three beats per measure. Use relaxed, legato strokes to achieve maximum tone. The dynamic contrasts are subtle and require concentration and careful balance. The fermata roll in the last measure should be long and, as indicated, "dying away" *(morendo)*. Use soft sticks.

Record your practice time for each day of the week.

Lesson Day	1	2	3	4	5	6		Total Practice Time
							=	

42

This study requires both aggressive staccato and relaxed legato playing. Consider each passage and select the appropriate type of stroke. Check the tuning carefully since this is an unusual interval for timpani. Use general purpose sticks.

Record your practice
time for each day of
the week.

Lesson Day	1	2	3	4	5	6		Total Practice Time
							=	

Record your practice
time for each day of
the week.

Begin the preparation of this study by first learning to sing the entire piece. Once the student can "hear" the piece mentally, tuning will be greatly simplified. Count carefully and make sure that none of the 5/8 measures are played in 6/8. Use general purpose or staccato sticks.

Record your practice time for each day of the week.

Lesson Day	1	2	3	4	5	6		Total Practice Time
							=	

44

The three stroke ruff should be executed with three single strokes. This figure is usually played with a slight crescendo into the last note. Flams must be played more open than on snare drum. Experiment with both figures before beginning this page. Use general purpose sticks.

The *forte-piano* roll is an important timpani technique. It is played by striking the drum *forte,* allowing the sound to decay to *piano* and then beginning the *piano* roll. The attack of the *piano* roll should not be heard. Master the *forte-piano* roll before beginning this study. Use general purpose sticks.

A-E

Record your practice time for each day of the week.

Lesson Day	1	2	3	4	5	6		Total Practice Time
							=	

46

Count this piece carefully so that the 7/8 measures are not accidentally played as 3/4 or 4/4. Do not "cheat" the short rolls by playing them too short; they should sound full and even. The opening *forte* should not be so loud that the *fortissimo* in measure 28 is unattainable. Use general purpose sticks.

A-D

Record your practice time for each day of the week.

Lesson Day	1	2	3	4	5	6		Total Practice Time
							=	

This study requires a subtle difference between the *mezzo-forte* dynamic level and the many recurring accents. **Accents must be played in relation to the dynamic level in which they occur. Do not overplay the accents. Use staccato sticks.**

C-F

Record your practice time for each day of the week.

Lesson Day	1	2	3	4	5	6		Total Practice Time
							=	

Teacher's Notes